South Korea

NORTH AMERICA

EUROPE

ASIA

AFRICA

SOUTH AMERICA

AUSTRALIA

Fred Martin

Heinemann
LIBRARY

First published in Great Britain by Heinemann Library
Halley Court, Jordan Hill, Oxford OX2 8EJ
a division of Reed Educational and Professional Publishing Ltd

Heinemann is a registered trademark of Reed Educational and Professional Publishing Ltd

OXFORD FLORENCE PRAGUE MADRID ATHENS
MELBOURNE AUCKLAND KUALA LUMPUR SINGAPORE TOKYO
IBADAN NAIROBI KAMPALA JOHANNESBURG GABORONE
PORTSMOUTH NH (USA) CHICAGO MEXICO CITY SAO PAULO

Designed by AMR
Illustrations by Art Construction
Printed in Hong Kong / China

03 02 01 00 99
10 9 8 7 6 5 4 3 2 1

ISBN 0 431 04557 7

British Library Cataloguing in Publication Data

Martin, Fred, 1948-
  Step Into South Korea
  1. Korea (South) – Geography – Juvenile literature
  I.Title II.South Korea
  915.1'95

This book is also available in hardback (ISBN 0 431 04556 9).

Acknowledgements
The Publishers would like to thank the following for permission to reproduce photographs:
Aspect Pictures, J. Alex Langley, p.14; Colorific Photo Library, Kari Ahlberg/Lehtikuva Oy, p.27
Martti Kainulainen/Lehtikuva Oy, p.22, John Nordell/JB Pictures, p.28, Michael Yamashita, pp.18, 19, 24, 25; Hutchison Library, Michael Macintyre, p.20, Andrew Sole, pp.6, 15; Panos Pictures, Jim Holmes, pp.5, 7, 8, 23; Trip Photo Library, T. Bognor, p.29, R. Nichols, p.10, Trip, pp.4, 9, 11, 12, 13, 16, 17, 21, 26

Cover photographs: Korea National Tourist Commission and Panos Pictures

Our thanks to Betty Root for her comments in the preparation of this book.

Every effort has been made to contact holders of any material reproduced in this book. Any omissions will be rectified in subsequent printings if notice is given to the Publisher.

There are some deciduous forests on the mountains where it is too high and too steep for farming. Coniferous trees grow where it is coldest.

ANIMALS

There are not many deer or other big animals left living in the wild in South Korea. There are many smaller animals, such as shrews, and birds including woodpeckers.

About half of all the rain in Seoul falls in June and July.

TOWNS AND CITIES

THE CAPITAL CITY

There have been cities in South Korea for at least 1000 years. The ancient rulers built palaces, temples and tombs in these cities. Some of these buildings are still there. Seoul is the **capital city** of South Korea. It was chosen as a capital city about 550 years ago. Some buildings in the city are very old. The Kyongbok Palace was built in 1395.

Seoul is lit up at night by the lights from shops, offices and cars. There are mountains on three sides of the city.

MODERN SEOUL

Most buildings in Seoul are modern **high-rise** office blocks, shops, factories and flats. The highest building is 63 floors high. Some roads are on stilts. There is an underground railway called a **metro**.

OTHER CITIES

There are about 40 big cities in South Korea. Pusan on the south coast is the country's biggest sea port. New factories have been built in many of the cities. The cities have grown quickly because people have come to work in the cities' offices and factories.

This is a department store in Seoul. People use the buses and cars to get about in the city.

Seoul is almost completely surrounded by mountains. South Koreans believe that this is the best kind of place to build a city.

11

A CITY FAMILY

THE SHIN FAMILY HOME

The Shin family lives on the edge of the city of Seoul. Mr and Mrs Shin have two boys. Yongsu is eleven years old and Yongsok is eight. The family live on the fourth floor of a tall block of flats.

THE DAY'S WORK

Mr Shin works for a company that makes cars. He usually goes to work by car. He leaves at 6.30am and gets home late. Mrs Shin helps in an old people's home. She also cooks and cleans for her family.

The block of flats where the Shin family live.

Mr Shin works in an office in the centre of Seoul. He uses computers to help do his work.

Mrs Shin and her two sons in a local supermarket.

THE CHILDREN'S DAY

The two boys go to the same school. Many of the classes have 40 children in them. After school, the boys go home and do their homework. When they play, they enjoy meeting their friends for ball games or to go roller-skating. After dinner, they watch television or play board games.

Yongsu in his art class at school.

The Shin family sit at a low table for their evening meal.

FARMING AND FISHING

CROPS AND ANIMALS

There is not much flat land for farming in South Korea. Most farms are very small. Farmers grow rice, maize, soybeans, cabbage, peppers, melons and different types of fruit. Some keep pigs, cattle and chickens. They also keep silk worms for their fine threads of silk.

Some farmers still use animals to do the ploughing.

GROWING RICE

Rice is the main crop in South Korea. Rice grows where the weather is warm and wet. The rice fields have to be flooded with water. Rice fields are called **paddy fields**. Low mud walls around the fields keep the water in.

FISHING

Fishing is very important because there is so little land for farming. People catch squid, tuna and most other types of fish. Some fishing boats travel thousands of kilometres to their **fishing grounds**.

About 30 years ago, about half the people worked in farming. Now there are not nearly so many. This is because there are better paid jobs in offices and factories.

Some fishing boats tied up in a fishing port. South Koreans eat many types of fish such as squid and tuna.

A FISHING FAMILY

The Han family outside their home.

Mrs Han waves goodbye to Mr Han as he sets sail.

THE HAN FAMILY

Han Yong-san is a fisherman. He lives with his wife Ok-hee in a small fishing village. They have a son called Yong-ho who is fifteen years old. The meanings of people's names are important in South Korea. Yong-ho means someone who stands tall and is strong.

A DAY AT SEA

On most days, Mr Han goes to sea in his fishing boat. He leaves in the afternoon and does not come back until the next morning. He sells the fish at a local market as soon as he gets back. Then he goes home to have breakfast. Sometimes Mrs Han cooks a meal of boiled flatfish with red pepper.

Mrs Han buying food.

Mrs Han is cooking breakfast.

AT SCHOOL WITH YONG-HO

Yong-ho goes to school in the village. He likes learning English and maths. He is good at the **martial arts** sport of *tae'kwondo*. He wants to join the police when he leaves school.

Yong-ho in his bedroom.

MARKETS AND SHOPS

This scene is inside a department store in Seoul.

LIVING IN CITIES

More than half the people in South Korea live in cities. They buy what they need in shops and in street markets. They can afford to buy the best food and clothes. They also earn enough to buy television sets, computers and other electrical goods.

A street market in Seoul. There are many markets like this in the cities.

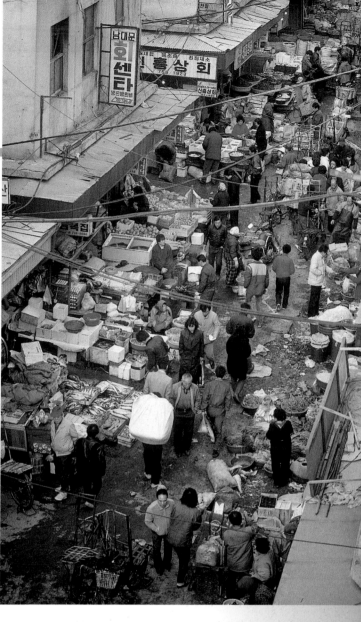

MARKETS

Early every morning, the farmers send their food to big markets in the cities. Shop and restaurant owners buy the food there and sell it to their customers.

CITY SHOPPING

The biggest and most expensive shops are in Seoul and the other cities. There are department stores and shops in modern shopping malls. Some people still like to visit street markets. They can buy television sets, clothes and almost anything else. Some of the goods in markets come straight from factories. They are cheaper than in the shops.

The Namdaemun market in Seoul is one of the biggest markets in the city.

19

SOUTH KOREAN FOOD

COOKING RICE

Rice is part of most meals in South Korea. It is boiled or fried, either on its own or mixed with eggs, vegetables or pieces of fish.

Different types of food are cooked and sold in street markets.

SPICY FOOD

People in South Korea eat all kinds of vegetables. One favourite meal is *kimch'i*. It is made from cabbage with peppers and garlic. Spices with strong hot flavours, like ginger, are added to many cooked meals. Meat is usually cut into small chunks or strips. It is either fried in an open pan or grilled over a barbecue. One barbecued meal with meat is called *pulgogi* which means 'fire dish'.

EATING RULES

All the different foods cooked for one meal are put on the table together. They can be eaten in any order. People use spoons for soup, but usually eat everything else with chopsticks. Everyone waits until the oldest person starts to eat. Nobody leaves the meal until the oldest person has finished.

Young people sometimes go to McDonalds or to pizza restaurants for meals.

Meals are often eaten from a low table. People sit cross-legged on the floor.

MADE IN SOUTH KOREA

FAMOUS NAMES

You may have something in your home that was made in South Korea. Samsung is a South Korean company that makes electrical goods, such as televisions and computers. Daewoo and Hyundai make cars.

Making cars using robots. Cars from South Korea are sold in many countries.

TOP TEN

South Korea has only made modern goods to sell to other countries in the past 30 years. Now it is in the world's top ten countries for making ships, cars and tyres. Clothes, chemicals and most other types of goods are also made in South Korea.

One company in South Korea has built one new ship every three weeks for the last fifteen years.

SOLD ABROAD

At first, the people in factories worked hard for low wages. The goods were bought by people in other countries. This brought money into South Korea and helped to make the country more wealthy. Workers now earn more and are better off.

Making television sets in a factory. Why do you think the worker is wearing gloves?

TRANSPORT

ROADS AND TRAINS

There is every kind of modern transport in South Korea. There are motorways and other main roads called expressways. These go between all the main towns and cities. There are trains for passengers and **freight**. Trains are a good way to carry heavy goods, like cars. There are high-speed trains between the biggest cities.

There are many different ways to get about in the cities.

Many people travel to work by train. This is an electric train.

AIRPORTS

The country's main airport is in Seoul. It is called Kimpo airport. Some flights are to and from other countries. Others are flights between the cities in South Korea. South Korea needs a new airport because so many people want to travel by air.

FERRY BOATS

People can go by ferry along the coast or to the islands. The fastest journey by sea is in a special type of boat called a hydrofoil. Most of the rivers are not deep enough for boats. Factory goods are taken by ships to other countries.

An aircraft takes off or lands every two minutes at Seoul's Kimpo airport.

ARTS AND SPORTS

ANCIENT ARTS

South Korea has an ancient history of music, dancing and poetry. The people loved to perform these in the palaces and in the villages. Many people liked to do beautiful handwriting using a brush. This is called **calligraphy**. It is now becoming a popular hobby for people in South Korea.

This choir and orchestra play music from the ancient courts and palaces.

MUSIC AND DANCE

Traditional South Korean music is made with gongs, drums and stringed instruments. Dancers wear masks or colourful costumes. They dance slowly, sometimes balancing on one foot.

FIGHTING SPORTS

South Korea has its own form of **martial arts**, called *tae'kwondo*. Many South Koreans enjoy watching and playing football, basketball and baseball.

The football World Cup will be held in South Korea and Japan in AD2002. Matches will be played in both countries.

Tae'kwondo is a fighting sport from South Korea. The word *tae'kwondo* means foot, fist and way.

FESTIVALS AND CUSTOMS

WAYS OF CONFUCIUS

Confucius was a famous Chinese teacher who lived about 2500 years ago. Many people in South Korea still try to follow his teaching. He said that young people must always obey older people and that everyone must obey their rulers.

These men are taking part in a Confucian ceremony.

There are many old village dances and other performances. They celebrate weddings and special times for farming.

LOCAL FESTIVALS

There are many village festivals. One is a tug-of-war between different villages. Another is a battle between monsters made by the villagers. The winning team has good luck and a good harvest.

MOONS AND MONTHS

Dates used to be worked out by the positions of the moon. Most festivals are still held at special positions of the moon. The harvest celebrations are always held on the fifteenth day of the eighth moon.

A PROUD PAST

South Koreans are very proud of their ancient festivals and customs.

The main religions in South Korea are Buddhism and Christianity.

SOUTH KOREA FACTFILE

People

People from South Korea are called South Koreans.

Capital city

The **capital city** of South Korea is Seoul.

Largest cities

Seoul is the largest city, with nearly eight-and-a-half million people. The second largest city is Pusan and Taegu is the third largest city.

Head of country

South Korea is ruled by a president and a **government**.

Population

There are over 200 million people living in South Korea.

Money

The money in South Korea is called the won (W).

Language

The language spoken in South Korea is Korean.

Religion

Most people in South Korea are Buddhist or Christian and a few are Confucianist.